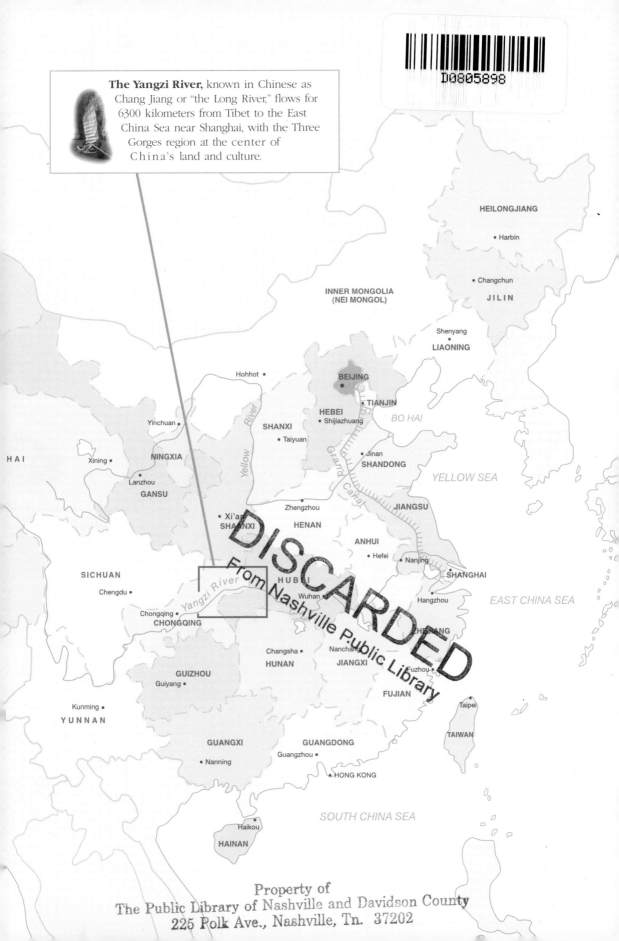

THREE GORGES OF THE
YANGZI
GRAND CANYONS OF CHINA

GRAND CANYONS OF CHINA

You have seen classic Chinese paintings of fantastic steep mountains amidst dreamy clouds. Rushing waters frothing below towering peaks. A lone fisherman adrift in the flow, dwarfed by the majestic scenery. People struggling to survive in a beautiful but cruel environment. For centuries, this image—the fabled Three Gorges of the Yangzi River in central China—has fired the imagination of artists and travelers. Here is a region that must be seen and experienced to be believed: this immense river, greater in volume than the entire Mississippi, winds through a mountain gorge as vast as the Grand Canyon of Arizona.

People have struggled for thousands of years to navigate the treacherous rapids of the Three Gorges and safely pass through this land of majestic perils. The poet Li Bai recounted his arduous passage by junk over a thousand years ago: "Traveling to Sichuan is more difficult than climbing to Heaven." The roiling waters of the Gorges continues to swallow unfortunate local boatmen who meet the "river dragon". The Great River is full of their *shui gui*, "water ghosts", both ancient and all too fresh.

Today the Three Gorges are undergoing a vast transformation with the contruction of the world's largest hydroelectric dam project, which will raise a vast reservoir and displace 1.5 million local residents. This edition presents many stunning views of the Gorges as a final farewell before inundation casts the region into an uncertain future.

Cover and title page *Above the banks of the meandering river tower the layered peaks of the Gorges celebrated by poets since ancient times. The haunting beauty of a lonely boat floating on the luminous waters of the river and poised against those peaks, their gaunt and rugged silhouette softened by swirling mists, remains the stuff of poetry today.*

Opposite *Details from traditional painting depicting the Three Gorges.*

Below *In former times, teams of strong men used to pull bamboo hawsers to haul junks up the perilous rapids along this tracker trail in the Qutang Gorge.*

LAND & WATERS

The Yangzi River is central to China's geography, long history, and deep cultural heritage. The main waterway through the heart of China, from Tibet to Shanghai, the Yangzi bustles with the traffic of the river valley's 450 million residents. Thousands of boats, from small craft to barges and passenger liners, ply the river's main channel and its tributaries and canals, crowding the docks of innumerable villages and cities. Life along these shores is truly afloat, from the sampan rafts of fishermen to the luxuriously appointed cruisers carrying international travelers to the region's scenic and cultural wonders.

The Yangzi River gathers from glacial waters on the Tibetan Plateau, flows south and east, gathering power as its tumbling tributaries burst through the mountain ranges of Amdo, once the eastern province of Tibet, then splashes down into the Sichuan Basin. Four large rivers converge to squeeze through the Gorges before wandering another 2000 kilometers east to the sea near Shanghai. In the Gorges, where swirling torrents scour the river bed, the Yangzi is the world's deepest river at some 150 meters, carrying millions of tons of rock from Tibet and silt from the vast muddy terraces of Sichuan. The Gorges are the funnel for this great erosion, accelerated in recent decades by widespread deforestation along the steep slopes of eastern Tibet. The Yangzi's upper tributaries, the Min and Dadu, have become clogged with giant logs from old-growth trees that tumble down into these suddenly muddy rivers. Vast rafts once floated down the Yangzi to market, with caretaker's cabins built over the lashed logs. Now the harvest—what timber remains—travels by train to China's booming cities. Meanwhile, the Yangzi carries millions of tons of erosion out to sea.

Opposite *Traffic in the Wu Gorge. Most local boats have engines but lack radio or radar. The traditional boatmen's flamboyant shouts echo in the Gorges.*

Inset *A man pauses for a taste of local tobacco in a river town market. Farmers come down to the Yangzi—the highway of central China—to trade produce and see the world passing by.*

Below *Scissors Peak towers over a river cruiser in the Wu Gorge.*

Above *The Yangzi's glacial source on Mount Geladandong in the Kunlun range of the Qinghai-Tibet plateau, 6621 meters above sea level. These waters gather and flow some 6300 kilometers before reaching the East China Sea near the port city of Shanghai.*

In the Mesozoic Era some 100 million years ago, the upper Yangzi flowed west into the primordial Mediterranean. The Indian subcontinent collided with Asia, causing the Himalayas to rise to their present height. The Sichuan Basin filled with waters from surrounding mountains to become a vast sea. The land was pressed down by the water's great weight, deepening the basin and enriching the sea bed with silt. The mountain ranges along the eastern rim of the Sichuan Sea are sedimentary limestone uplift, jagged remnants of an earlier seabed. Water has undermined the soft rock and backcut between valleys, causing dramatic turns in the river course. Over thousands of years, the water worked its way between the ranges and roared in an immense rush through the last range toward the East China Sea. The inundation scoured the land, creating a vast plain that remains at high risk for flooding to this day.

The Yangzi drops precipitously from its source in northern Tibet to the Sichuan Basin, descending 90 percent of its altitude. As the mighty current reaches Chongqing, the Yangzi has fallen to only 200 meters above sea level with 2500 kilometers still to flow to the sea. After rushing through the Gorges, the river meanders with an average depth of six meters, depositing silt that extends the delta a kilometer every century.

Just downstream from Nanjin Pass at the city of Yichang, the Jiang Han plain opens out into broad flatlands. The Yangzi wanders through a vast and central valley, the "land of fish and rice" that is the heart of China. The levee banks spread wide to hold the river as it wends its way east over shallows, around low mud islands, and through vast wetlands. During low water season from fall through winter, the current is barely discernible. The Yangzi makes its way to the sea partly by the pressure of upstream water forcing slack water ahead.

Above *The high water mark of the flood of 1931 in downtown Wuhan is a vivid reminder to millions of residents who are threatened by the annual flooding in the Jiang Han plain downstream of the Gorges.*

Below *A sampan—literally a "three logs" craft—emerges from a clear tributary into the great muddy mainstream of the Yangzi, which carries silt caused by deforestation in Tibet and intensive agriculture in Sichuan.*

Not long ago, it was an arduous sail and dangerous haul upstream to reach Sichuan. Nowadays most travelers fly into the new airport outside of Chongqing, the "Mountain City" and ancient port at the confluence of the Jialing River and the Yangzi, which has made it the transportation hub of Southwest China. Chongqing is now officially the largest city in China—and the world—with some 30 million residents in a new governmental district formed from eastern Sichuan Province and including the legendary Three Gorges region.

INTO THE GORGES

From "Alarm at First Entering the Gorges"

Above, a mountain ten thousand feet high:
Below, a river a thousand fathoms deep.
A strip of sky, walled by cliffs of stone;
Wide enough for the passage of a single reed.
At Qutang, a straight cleft yawns.
At Yen-yu, islands block the stream.
Long before night the walls are black with dusk.
Without wind white waves rise.
The big rocks are like a flat sword.
The little rocks resemble ivory tisks.
Frail and slender, the twisted bamboo rope:
Weak, the dangerous hold of the towers' feet.
A single slip, the whole convoy lost:
And my life hangs on this thread!

Bai Juyi (772—846)

Most travelers to the Gorges board river boats docked to floating barges on the muddy banks of the river in Chongqing. From here the Yangzi flows east for 650 kilometers through the Gorges to the

Nanjin Pass at Yichang in Hubei Province. Along this course, the lush banks of the Yangzi are sown with a variety of vegetables. In terraces above the shore are grown corn, orange groves and mulberry trees to raise silk worms. "Anything that is dropped will grow" is an old expression extolling the legendary fertility of the land of Sichuan. The climate is moist and semitropical yet cool in winter. Siberian winds blow high over the mountains, while the river runs warm and becomes shrouded in dense fog. The sun shines so rarely that when it returns in the spring, it is said dogs bark to chase it away.

Above *Navigation along the Great River is still a hands-on skill. Nowadays the "dragon in the river" is the congested traffic along the world's busiest waterway.*

WHITE KING CITY

At Kuimen, the "mighty gate" entrance of the Qutang Gorge, a prominent hill overlooks the high cliffs. In the first century B.C., Gong Sun Shu, a king of Shu (now Sichuan), built a stronghold to guard the passage. A well on the hill once emitted a white vapor in the shape of a dragon. Taking this as a good omen from heaven, the king called himself the White

King and to this day the site is called Baidi Cheng—White King City. Today there is a small temple with life-size, brightly painted sculptural dioramas of the Three Kingdom Period. At this site in the third century A.D. King Liu Bei put up his futile defense against the attacking forces of Wu. The dying Liu Bei left his kingdom to his trusted minister Zhu Geliang, who in an enduring testament of loyalty agreed only to be regent to the king's young son.

White King City is also famous as a site where poets have gathered over the centuries and left a legacy inscribed in stone steles. The array of tablets in open air pavilion halls are renowned in Chinese literature, including the "Bamboo Leaf Poem" which is engraved in the form of the plant's leaves.

Below this garden of culture, the angry waters of the Yangzi rush into the Qutang Gorge. In rocks at the foot of the hill still stand iron posts from the Song Dynasty (twelfth century A.D.) that were used to chain the river for defense and to stop traffic for taxation. The nearby walled town of Fengjie once raised more funds for the Imperial coffers than any other site in China.

Opposite *Sedan chairs hike up to Baidi Cheng ("White King City"), overlooking the Qutang Gorge. This third century B.C. fortress is famous in history and literature for the poems extolling the dramatic view. In the Song Dynasty (twelfth century A.D.) the river was barred with chains across the rapids, and high taxes were charged to any junks that passed. This hill site will become an island in the Three Gorges Dam reservoir.*

QUTANG GORGE

The mighty Qutang Gorge is the shortest of the Three Gorges at eight kilometers, and the narrowest at 55 meters across. But its cliffs are the highest, towering 1250 meters above the river at the triumphant spire of Red Shield Peak. At the Kuimen narrows of the Qutang Gorge entrance, there once stood a gigantic rock Yan Yu—called the Great Goose—which split the roaring river and would smash unwary boats. The Qutang is still a giant chute of jostling, churning water whose whirlpools and spreading swells toss even large boats aside against the sheer banks. Above the waters, tracker trails were cut into the cliffs where hundreds of

Below *A navigation control station in the Qutang Gorge, now radio-equipped to control passage in the narrow channel.*

Opposite *A classic pavilion overlooks the Qutang Gorge.*

Right *Calligraphy cliff in Qutang Gorge. The inscription reads: "At the Mighty Gate of Kuimen only the bravest of boatmen under heaven dare pass."*

Right inset *Rhinoceros Viewing the Moon rock formation in Qutang Gorge.*

Below *A navigation control station with one-way arrow markers for traffic in the Qutang Gorge. This system was established by British customs officials to provide safe passage when the first steamboats came up the Gorges in the 1890s.*

men once heaved on bamboo hawsers to haul junks up the rapids. In flood season, the waters can rise 50 or more meters, and the hydraulic forces are barely mastered even by today's powerful engines. Sand and rocky debris are thrown up into the current as *fei sha* —"flying sand" — that can break a wooden boat apart in a flash. In former times, one of every seven boats was lost to the rapids. Travelers used to express their fear and respect of the waters with offerings made in a multitude of shrines to appease the river dragon and allow safe passage. Now the passage is a routine and magnificent photo-op from aboard the river liners that pass every day.

On the south cliff face, calligraphic carvings remain from centuries ago, where once stood a classic tea house, now washed away by recent flooding. Recent inscriptions include: "These great gorges kept out the Japanese pirates!" and the once popular slogan "Long Live Chairman Mao." Further down the Gorge, a rock formation on a ridge is called Rhinoceros Viewing the Moon. As one passes the scene, the rock turns face and transforms into King Liu Bei Sitting on His Throne.

The Qutang Gorge opens out abruptly into the broad valley of Daxi, a fertile farming land with terraced slopes full of fragrant orange trees. This more hospitable landscape is a site of archeological research by Guo Moruo, who discovered evidence of a Stone Age people predating the Peking Man of North China. Other evidence recently discovered in caves of Wushan County has helped confirm the Gorges as an early cradle of human development in Asia.

WU GORGE

Above *Goddess Peak, in the Wu Gorge, rises above the most treacherous turn of the Yangzi River. The journey was deemed safe whenever travelers were able to view and make offerings to the stone pillar of the Goddess Yao Ji. If rain or clouds covered her figure, it was said she was bathing, and her modesty was to be respected.*

The Wu Gorge is the greatest chasm of the Yangzi, deep and mysterious with sweeping flanks of rock rising to twelve holy peaks that tower up to 1200 meters over the rushing waters. The river course turns at sharp angles giving the impression that there is no way though these rugged mountains. The region was named after the legendary Sorceress Wu, who first provided herbal medicine to an ancient emperor. The mountains above the Wu Gorge are still combed for several types of rare plants that rank among the most potent in Chinese pharmacology. Of the twelve peaks overlooking the great chasm of the Wu Gorge, the most famous is the Goddess Peak. Atop the summit is a 35-meter high pillar of stone, said to bear the likeness of the goddess Yao Ji, which stands 750 meters above the twisted channel of the river. Gorge eagles soar on uplifts of air and dive for fish and refuse in the swirling waters. In former times, the Goddess Peak was the object of prayer and offerings by boatmen and passengers for safe passage on the Great River. Today a glimpse of her is still considered good luck.

Just downstream from the Goddess Peak, on the north bank, is a large hollow in the cliff known as the Kong Ming Tablet, dating to the Three Kingdoms era (third century A.D.). When soldiers of the Kingdom of Wu pursued Prime Minister Zhu Geliang and the defenders of the Kingdom of Shu up the Gorges, Zhu inscribed on the rock face the oath of loyalty which the Wu general Sun Quan had vowed yet broken. When

Sun Quan saw his own words written by his former ally, his honor was touched and he called back his army out of the Gorges.

THE SMALL GORGES & HINTERLANDS

The river port of Wushan is at the entrance of the Wu Gorge, set at the confluence of the Daning River tributary. Fleets of sampans make the journey from the floating docks of Wushan up the Daning into the Small Three Gorges and beyond to ever more narrow gorges. This trip into the inner canyons reveals spectacular cliffs and dramatic landscapes. In these canyons, the life of the subsistence farmers and boatmen has changed little over the centuries. The people of the ancient Ba Kingdom once inhabited this remote region over two thousands years ago. Ba nobles were entombed in large wooden coffins with a slave woman who was

Below *Wushan harbor at dusk. This river town is a traditional stopping point for boats after braving the dangers of the Qutang and Wu Gorges. The peak over the channel is Wu Mountain, named for the legendary Sorceress Wu, a healer who brought herbal medicine to an ancient emperor.*

Inset *A villager of Qing Shi in the Wu Gorge draws from the Yangzi for use at home, well boiled.*

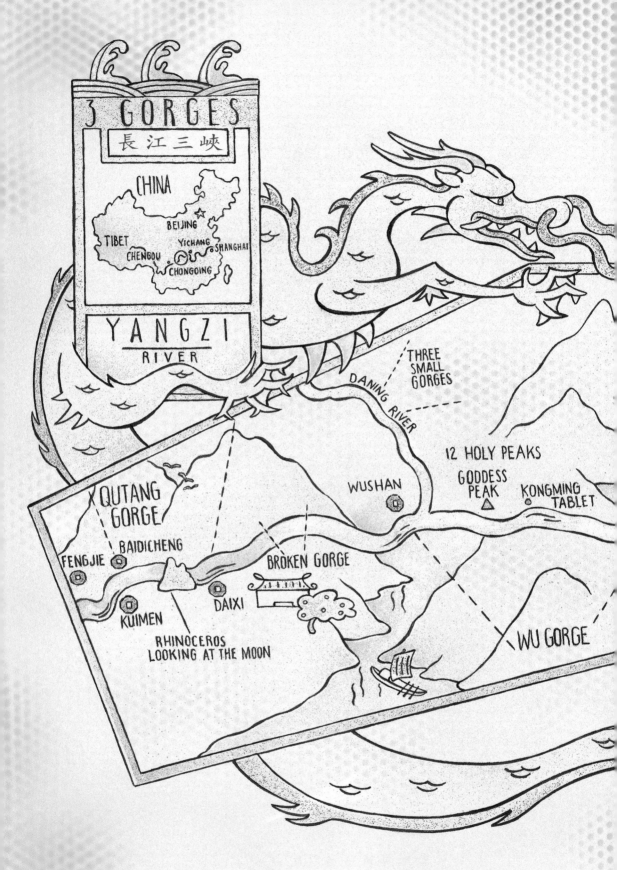

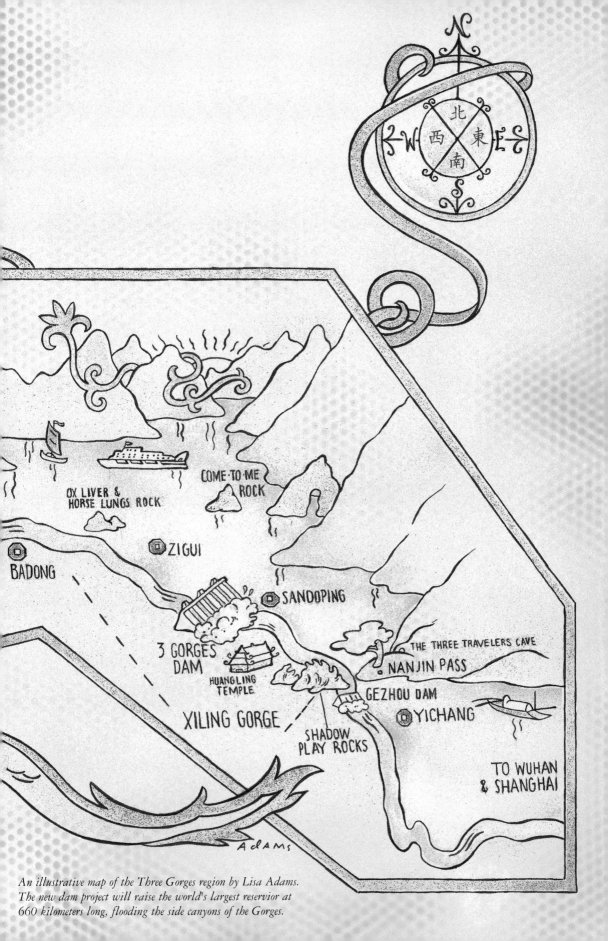

An illustrative map of the Three Gorges region by Lisa Adams.
The new dam project will raise the world's largest reservoir at
660 kilometers long, flooding the side canyons of the Gorges.

sacrificed to be a nursemaid in the afterlife. The coffins were suspended in cliff crevices, and some remain visible perched high in the narrow gorges. In past centuries, wooden walkways were built along the gorge cliffs of the Daning for access into the highlands and beyond. The traditional trade item was salt, mined in the cliffs and sold at a high profit in the ancient capital of Xian far to the north. In times of turmoil, these wooden walkways could be burnt away to halt the advance of invaders. Square peg holes may still be seen high above the stream.

The town of Dachang, at a broad bend north of the Small Three Gorges in the valley of the Daning, was once a prosperous trading center in the Ming Dynasty (fourteenth to seventeenth centuries). Marble steps rise from the river through an entrance arch of the old town walls, which are now mostly dismantled. The stones from the wall were used to make a breakwater against floods in the Mao years, when deforestation was ordered, resulting in loss of hill cover. Monuments and family tombstones were mixed with cement to form the dike. Stately brick and wooden homes of merchants still stand along lanes paved in stone. The residents, mostly farmers who till the rich alluvial soil deposited by seasonal floods, are busier than ever digging terraces above the expected reservoir level. Baskets full of nutrient-rich bottom soil are now being carried up the steep hills to enrich the terraces.

Above *A traditional wooden boat with a bamboo thatch cover, a familiar sight on the Daning River tributary.*

Opposite *One of the last sailing junks in the region passes under the Wu Dou or "No Struggle" Bridge, built in the Wu Gorge during Ming Dynasty in the sixteenth century.*

Inset *This Ba people coffin, once suspended in a crevice high above the Yangzi River, is now in the Three Gorges Museum in Wanxian.*

Below *Goddess Peak, in the Wu Gorge.*

Left *A reconstructed traditional walkway along the Daning River. In ancient times, the Ba people would repel invaders by setting fire to the walkway.*

Below *The Kong Ming Tablet, in the Wu Gorge, is the site of an ancient calligraphy inscription by Zhu Geliang, Prime Minister of the Kingdom of Shu in the Three Kingdoms Period (third century* A.D.*).*

Opposite *The Lotus Pavilion Peak towers above the Emerald Gorge of the Daning River. A canyon terrace above the stream is called Guan Yin Tai or the Seat of the Goddess of Mercy. Monkeys swing in the lush bamboo brush laced with waterfalls cascading from the heights.*

How long can these poor farmers survive in these hills after their "good earth," the source of their sustenance, is drowned?

In this backcountry of Badong County live some 150,000 Tujia people, an indigenous minority whose Chinese name means "earth home." Perhaps descendants of the Ba people, they are now subsistence farmers who build houses in high, steep terrain where only corn and tobacco can grow. They derive cash income by collecting herbal plants and hunting wild game in the highlands. Now that roads have been cut through the region, the traditional Tujia elegant wooden boats are put to use for tourists to enjoy floating down to the narrow canyons of the Shennong Stream. The Tujia are a cheerful people who sing haunting melodies that echo in the mountains. Visitors are expected to return a song and, when in the villages, join in the folk dances which imitate bird movements.

An interesting custom of the Tujia is the practice of elopement, whereby a young man stages a kidnapping of his chosen young girl, who must make a great display of crying to show her loyalty to her parents. If the girl cries well enough, the family grants permission to marry her abductor.

Ever steeper ridges rise above the Tujia region to Shennongjia, a mountain basin 3000 meters above sea level, a region famous as the source of Chinese herbs. Shennong, or "Spirit of Agriculture," the mythical founder of Chinese medicine, hiked these mountains and brought the

Right *The gate into Dachang, a well-preserved Ming Dynasty town in Wushan County, once a center of China's salt trade. When the waters rise behind the Three Gorges Dam, the walled town will be flooded. A few of the 500-year-old houses are scheduled to be moved upland.*

Opposite *Canoes of the Tujia people along Shennong Stream in Badong County. These elegant wooden craft are poled down the Tiger Rapids to the Yangzi as the boatmen's plaintive songs echo in the towering canyons.*

knowledge of plants to the Chinese nation. Up above sheer, razor-like cliffs are slopes full of arrow bamboo, once the domain of pandas before they were hunted out. The region is now designated a World Biological Region to protect its remaining unique plants. The *hai wang,* or "sea nest," is considered a prime herb for its potency and many uses in traditional pharmacology. Its fibrous root is similar in shape to a sea anemone, and locals claim this as proof that the region was once under water. There are also many Crustaceous Era fossils from the ancient seas in the steep, rapidly eroding cliffs. In addition to medicinal herbs, Shennongjia is famous for its bears, foxes, rabbits, and birds that take on white coloring in the snowy winters. The dangers to human visitors are legendary, including vapors that can suffocate humans—likely swamp gas in its swampy hollows. "Man-eating trees" are said to have mangrove-like tentacles which, in times of drought, will grab animals as they pass and suck out their life fluids.

Most famous of the Shennongjia legends is the *ye ren,* a yeti-like primate, that stands nine feet tall,

Above *Corn racks hang from the ceiling of the Zhang family home in Badong County. They are Tujia, subsistence farmers and herb gatherers indigenous to the Gorges. Their homes and ancestral tombs are to be inundated by the Three Gorges Dam reservoir, forcing them to move upland to an uncertain future.*

Above *Fishermen reach into the whirling eddies of Xiling Gorge.*

Below *Tujia boatmen on Shennong Stream haul their canoe upstream back home after a day's run down to the Yangzi.*

with reddish fur and a terrible odor. The creature is said to live in the brush and nests in trees, eating fruit and leaves. The *ye ren* is nocturnal and wary of humans and has been sighted only occasionally. One researcher has an extensive collection of footprints, hairballs, and droppings, but expeditions in recent years have failed to confirm the legends.

Xiling Gorge

The longest of the Gorges is the Xiling Gorge, which stretches from Badong to Yichang—over 100 kilometers of varied cliffs and rapids. This gorge was famous for its odd rock formations, shallows, and treacherous currents. One midstream boulder—now blasted away—was named "Come to Me" after the traditional boat pilots' order to steer right for the rock so as to avoid another just under the rushing froth. A foreign skipper in the nineteenth century overruled a local pilot's order and found out the true route the hard way when his boat was smashed. Numerous river towns along the Xiling, such as Zigui and Badong, which were once built up as military production centers, are now being relocated to higher ground in anticipation of the rise of the great dam reservoir.

Below the dam site is Huangling Temple, the oldest building in the Gorges, dating from the first century B.C., dedicated to the Emperor Da Yu,

Above *The modern* Three Kingdoms *river cruiser is styled after a third century* A.D. *Yangzi warship.*

Below *Horse Lung and Ox Liver stalactite formations on the north bank of Xiling Gorge were once used for target practice by passing gunboats. To ancient boatmen struggling in small craft through these waters, the curious rocks once held animistic powers.*

Below *A Victoria river cruiser in the Xiling Gorge, seen from old Zigui town, soon to be relocated across the river at a new site below the Three Gorges Dam.*

legendary inventor of dams and water control. Further downstream are the famous formations of the Shadow Play rocks, with fanciful profiles of the Monkey King and his loyal follower the Pig Monk. Natural arches, waterfalls, and slot canyons covered in jungle growth make for dramatic

sights. A sheer cliff on the north bank is topped with a modern statute of a flying Buddhist *apsara* angel. This is the only stretch of the Gorges which will survive the reservoir. Yet current development on the shore and quarries for construction mar the cliffs.

The Xiling Gorge ends at Nanjin Pass, upstream of the booming city of Yichang. Here, on a promontory ridge looking out into the broadening expanse of the Yangzi, is an ancient watchtower presided over by a giant statue of the Three Kingdoms hero Zhang Fei. Many a battle was fought to protect the Gorges from invaders, most recently with the Japanese. Now a cable car carries visitors over the river for a better view of the craggy mountains. The ridge of Nanjin Pass contains the Three Travelers' Cave, with its interior passages full of inscriptions of poets and officials proclaiming the hazardous beauties of the Gorges. The rapids of Nanjin Pass that once inspired poetry are now calmed by the Gezhou Dam a few kilometers below, which has raised the lower Xiling waters to a smooth stream.

Below *A dragon boat at Zigui, home of patriotic poet Qu Yuan. An annual feast and boat races are held in honor of this poet who, as a minister in the Kingdom of Lu in the sixth century* B.C., *tossed himself into the Miluo River tributary in protest against the corruption of the period. Qu Yuan's body is said to have been carried back to Zigui by river fish, and as a reward these fish receive annual offerings of zhong zi (sticky rice cakes).*

Overleaf *Nanjin Pass at Yichang, entrance to the Xiling Gorge, and the first rapids, now calmed by the Gezhou Dam. The cliffs hold ancient fortifications to defend the Kingdom of Shu during the Three Kingdoms Period (third century* A.D.*)*

Traditional Boatman's Song

I have no food, what shall I do?
Hi yeh! Hi yeh!
Those things I eat are now too few. Hi yah!
Nothing to eat! What shall I do? I'll tell you what.
Hi yeh! Hi yeh!
I'll drop a mountain in the pot.
Hi yah! Plenty to eat!

From "Swimming"

Now I am swimming across the great Yangzi.
Today I am at ease.
It was by a stream that the Master said,
"Thus do things flow away!"
Sails move with the wind.
Tortoise and snake are still.
Great plans are afoot.
The mountain goddess
If she is still there
Will marvel at a world so changed.

Mao Zedong

Above *"San Xia Er Guan — a view of the Three Gorges."*

THE GREAT DAM

In the Xiling Gorge 75 kilometers upstream from the port of Yichang, a broad valley opens at the former village of Sandouping where the world's largest hydroelectric dam is now under construction. This "Great Wall across the River" will rise more than 110 meters high and stretch 1.5 kilometers across the river course, creating a reservoir 660 kilometers upstream to the port of Chongqing. The Three Gorges Project was first proposed in 1919 by Sun Yat-sen in his plan for the modernization of China and the Yangzi Valley through flood control, improved navigation, and electrical generation. This remains the mandate of the project, which is now underway after decades of debate. Estimated cost was originally U.S. $15 billion, but the final amount may be many times that figure. Half of the estimated cost is related to relocating some 1.5 million people in the lands to be flooded by the Great Dam reservoir. The site of the dam was selected by an American research team in the 1930s as the most stable anticline upraise of igneous rock in a region of loose sedimentary geology. Mao Zedong himself chose the large single dam design over the recommended series of smaller structures in spite of greater cost and technical challenges. The project was studied repeatedly in the following decades and officially approved in 1992 by the National People's Congress under the advocacy of Premier Li Peng.

A monumental set of five giant locks, each over 30 meters high, is rising along the north bank and will carry two-way ship traffic up and over the Great Dam. The great "peaceful lake" of the reservoir will forever still the legendary rapids of the Gorges and provide access to previously isolated upland valleys. Flood control, electrical production and navigation improvement will transform the economy of the region and the lives of its residents with effects on the river ecology in the entire Yangzi Valley.

The greatest sacrifice will be plant and animal species unique to the Gorges, many of which are neither cataloged nor well researched. Among these are the native musk deer, the golden hair monkey, and the gorge eagles that fish in the turbulent waters. The rare giant salamander lives in side streams under rocks in clear water, growing up to a meter long. It is called the *wa wa yu* or "baby fish" for its tiny hands and the cry it gives out when caught. It is now a protected species, and the market price has risen so high as to doom the last of its kind even before upland streams are flooded with the polluted water of the main river.

The giant Yangzi sturgeon is the largest of this ancient species of ocean fish, growing up to five meters long. This scaled giant has spawned for millennia in mountain streams of the Gorges and far up to Tibet. Now, after more than fifteen years of the natural course of the river being blocked by the Gezhou Dam near Yichang, sturgeon returning to spawn are caught at the dam face by fishermen with heavy nets. The sturgeon

Below (left) Construction crews work around the clock on major projects in China. (center) A worker stands above the turbine complex at the Three Gorges Dam site in 1999. The geological stability of the broad valley at Sandouping in the Xiling Gorge made this a favorable site for the massive dam. (right) Massive locks will lift ships and barges 110 meters in five stages to reach the Dam reservoir, a 660-kilometer stretch through the Gorges to the port of Chongqing.

are being introduced to lower streams which may not be habitable, spelling doom for the species. No passage for fish is planned for the Three Gorges Dam, a decision which will result in the elimination of many other species of migrating river fish.

A major cultural sacrifice is expected in the flooding of hundreds of identified archaeological sites. Stone Age settlements near Daxi, Ba kingdom tombs, and Han to Tang period sites are scheduled to be inundated even before a full survey can be completed. The largest historic building to be drowned in the region is the Temple of Zhang Fei, the general of the Three Kingdoms Period (third century A.D.) who was betrayed by his own officers when they chopped off his head, and threw his body in the river. His head was reportedly kept in a vat of oil and would rise to tell fortunes—until an earthquake destroyed the original temple a few centuries ago. Today a rebuilt fanciful complex is a short ferry ride across from the town of Yunyang. At night, the Temple is aglow with the flashing lights of karaoke parties. The building is scheduled to be disassembled and moved to a new site on higher ground, albeit without the general's prophetic talking head.

Funds appropriated for archaeology have not been fully issued for fear of holding up the construction, and only salvage research is being undertaken. Meanwhile, local people dig and officials conspire. A recently unearthed four-foot-tall bronze "spirit tree" from Wushan County dating back to the Eastern Han dynasty (25 to 220 A.D.) was smuggled out to a collector in America. The Chinese government, while claiming to be protective of the heritage of China, is fending off the concerns of international archaeologists and its own experts as it speeds the project forward. The Chinese people may never know what heritage was lost amidst the rush of progress.

The fate of the Three Gorges now lies in

Below *Mining underway in Xiling Gorge to prevent collapse of the cliff when the reservoir rises behind the Three Gorges Dam. Landslides are common in the Gorges. In 1984, one buried half of Xintan, a nearby village.*

Left *The Huangling Temple at Sandouping, located just down river from the Three Gorges Dam, was founded in the Han Dynasy (first century B.C.). The temple is the oldest building in the Gorges, and dedicated to Emperor Da Yu, legendary inventor of flood control and irrigation. His legacy is invoked by the national leaders and engineers who promote the benefits of the great new dam in the Three Gorges.*

the hands of the former engineers who run China from the Communist Party headquarters of Zhongnanhai—the Imperial residence next to the Forbidden City in Beijing. The Three Gorges project is not undertaken lightly by the authorities, who struggle with the competing priorities of modern China. The demands of national energy supply, flood control, and business opportunities loom far larger in their judgment than the fate of the local indigenous people, cultural heritage, wildlife, or scenic wonders of the Gorges. Among the proposed alternatives to the high dam is a series of smaller dams along the tributaries of the Yangzi, or a series of low-rise dams at other points in the Gorges, either of which would be less costly in social, environmental, and financial terms. But the "Great Wall across the Yangzi" is as much a matter of national pride and monumentalism as engineering analysis. The government invokes the project as a patriotic effort by construction teams representing the military and all regions of China.

The powerful economic interests behind the Three Gorges Dam have prevailed over forces that might have preserved and protected this endangered region. Dai Qing, the courageous writer and critic of the project claims, "If the Three Gorges could speak, they would plead for mercy!"

Meanwhile, the Gorges waters roil free for a few more years as residents prepare for the Great Dam reservoir to fill in 2003 and begin a new chapter in the long history of this unique region of China.

Selected Bibliography

Bonavia, Judy. *The Yangzi River*. Hong Kong: Odyssey, 1995.

Dai Qing. *The River Dragon is Coming*. New York: M. E. Sharpe, 1998.

Hersey, John. *A Single Pebble*. New York: Knopf, 1939.

How Man Wong. *Exploring the Yangtze*. Hong Kong: Odyssey, 1994.

Lynn, Madeleine, editor. *The Yangzi River: The Wildest, Wickedest River in the World*. Hong Kong: Oxford University Press, 1997.

Van Slyke, Lyman. *Yangtze: Nature, History and the River*. Stanford University Press, 1988.

Winchester, Simon. *The River at the Center of the World*. New York: Henry Holt, 1996.

Worcester, G. R. G. *Junks and Sampans of the Yangtze*. Annapolis: Naval Institute Press, 1923.

Acknowledgments

The author thanks for their expertise and encouragement: Sigmund Shi, Li Xianrong, Deirdre Chetham, Madeleine Lynn, Elizabeth Childs-Johnson, Seymour and Audrey Topping, Lawrence Sullivan, Nancy Liu, and International Rivers Network.

Left *Calligraphy on scroll:*

Wild waters
tumble eastward
through misty mountains
in the springtime

A traditional brush painting in the shan sui *(mountains and water) style. This work is typical of folk art sold to travelers in river town markets in the Three Gorges region.*